States of Matter

EXPRESS EDITION

Carol Baldwin

www.raintreepublishers.co.uk
Visit our website to find out more information about **Raintree** books.

To order:
☎ Phone 44 (0) 1865 888113
🖹 Send a fax to 44 (0) 1865 314091
🖥 Visit the Raintree Bookshop at **www.raintreepublishers.co.uk** to browse our catalogue and order online.

First published in Great Britain by Raintree Publishers, Halley Court, Jordan Hill, Oxford, OX2 8EJ, part of Harcourt Education Ltd.
Raintree is a registered trademark of Harcourt Education Ltd.

Produced for Raintree Publishers by Discovery Books Ltd.
Editorial: Louise Galpine, Carol Usher, Charlotte Guillain, and Isabel Thomas
Design: Victoria Bevan, Keith Williams (sprout.uk.com Limited), and Michelle Lisseter
Picture Research: Maria Joannou and Alison Prior
Production: Duncan Gilbert and Jonathan Smith
Originated by Dot Gradations Ltd
Printed and bound in China
by South China Printing Company

ISBN 1 844 43381 1 (hardback)
09 08 07 06 05
10 9 8 7 6 5 4 3 2 1

ISBN 1 844 43684 5 (paperback)
09 08 07 06 05
10 9 8 7 6 5 4 3 2 1

British Library Cataloguing in Publication Data
Baldwin, Carol, 1943-
States of matter. – (Freestyle express. Material matters)
1. Matter – Juvenile literature 2. Solids – Juvenile literature
3. Liquids – Juvenile literature 4. Gases – Juvenile literature
541'.042

A full catalogue record for this book is available from the British Library.

This levelled text is a version of
Freestyle: Material Matters: States of Matter.

Photo acknowledgements
Page 4, Science Photo Library; 4/5, Robert Harding Picture Library; 5 top, 5 bott,26-27,29, 30, 36-37, 40-41, 43, Corbis; 5 mid, Art Directors & Trip/M Peters; ; 6, FLPA/M Newman; 6/7, Science Photo Library/Simon Lewis; 7, 8, 18, 21,22-23, 24, 35,38 right,Trevor Clifford; 8/9, Art Directors & Trip/B Turner; 9, Science Photo Library/S Fraser; 10, Corbis/ Mark E Gibson; 10/11, Corbis/Richard T Nowitz; 11, 12 left, Corbis/D Boone; 12 right, Science Photo Library/M Land; 13, Science Photo Library/Sheila Terry; 14, Art Directors & Trip/J Ellard; 14/15, Corbis/ Lindsay Hebberd; 15, Corbis/Sandy Felsenthal; 16, Science Photo Library/ Charles D Winters; 16/17, FLPA/M Thomas; 17, Anthony Blake Picture Library/C Sneddon; 18/19, Art Directors & Trip/R Drury 19, Comstock; 20, Corbis/Roger Ball; 20/21, Science Photo Library/TRL Ltd; 22, Art Directors & Trip/H Rogers; 23, Shout Pictures; The Skyscan Photolibrary/ C Claughton; 25, Robert Harding Picture Library/R Francis ; 26, Digital Vision; 27, John Cleare Mountain Photography; 28, Science Photo Library/M Burnett; 30/31, NASA/ Hubble Space Telescope Center; 31, Corbis/Douglas Mesney; 32, Robert Harding Picture Library/P Pebbles; 32/33, Art Directors & Trip/M Peters; 33, Corbis/David Stoecklein; 34, Art Directors & Trip/F Blackburn; 34/35, Science Photo Library/T Craddock; 36, Corbis/Jeffrey L Rotman; 38 left, Corbis/Ted Streshinsky; 39, Corbis/Bettmann; 40, FLPA/By Silvestris; 41, FLPA/Minden Pictures; 42, FLPA/J Bastable; 42/43, Robert Harding Picture Library/Lee Frost; 44, Corbis/Richard T Nowitz; 45, Science Photo Library/TRL Ltd.

Cover photograph of a plasma globe reproduced with permission of Science Photo Library/ Alfred Pasieka.

Every effort has been made to contact copyright holders of any material reproduced in this book. Any omissions will be rectified in subsequent printings if notice is given to the Publishers.

Disclaimer
All the Internet addresses (URLs) given in this book were valid at the time of going to press. However, due to the dynamic nature of the Internet, some addresses may have changed, or sites may have changed or ceased to exist since publication. While the author and Publishers regret any inconvenience this may cause readers, no responsibility for any such changes can be accepted by either the author or the Publishers.

Contents

Any words appearing in the text in bold, **like this**, are explained in the Glossary. You can also look out for some of them in the Word bank at the bottom of each page.

Up, up, and away

Imagine being in a hot-air balloon. You turn on the burner, which roars into life. The air in the balloon heats up. When the air is hot enough, the balloon rises off the ground.

Now you are high in the sky. You turn the burner off to stop the balloon rising.

Back to Earth

You choose a large, empty field to land in. You let some of the air out of the balloon. The balloon comes down. When it lands you let all the air out. The balloon **deflates** gently.

Why does the balloon rise when the burner is turned on? How does it come back down to the ground? To answer these questions you need to know how gases behave. Gas is a **state of matter**. Solids and liquids are also states of matter.

Find out later...

... how hot lightning is.

... if something has to be cold to **freeze**.

... why ice floats.

---

state of matter whether something is a solid, liquid, gas, or plasma

What is matter?

All materials are made from **matter**. Air, water, food, animals, and plants all contain matter. Matter is made of tiny **particles**. These are called **atoms**. Anything containing matter has **mass** and **volume**.

Mass

Mass is how much matter something has. The mass of an object is measured in grams or kilograms.

Volume

The amount of space an object takes up is its volume.

Tiny particles
This is a sand sculpture of a dragon. It is made of millions of tiny grains of sand. Every grain of sand is made up of atoms joined together.

This worker, the torch, and the air all have mass and volume. They are all types of matter.

Describing matter

Properties help us to describe matter. Colour, shape, and hardness are properties. They are physical properties. You can usually tell these by looking or measuring.

Chemical properties tell us how a material behaves in a **reaction** with something else. A chemical property of wood is that it can burn.

Comparing properties

To check if this liquid is water we can compare its properties to water's properties. Ice cubes float in water. The ice cubes in this picture have sunk. So the liquid cannot be water.

reaction chemical change that produces new substances

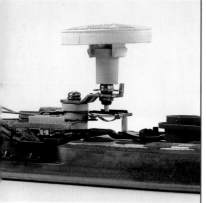

Thermostats are used to control the temperature of heaters. They work because the metals inside expand by different amounts.

Matter and energy

Matter exists in different forms. Usually it is:

- solid, for example ice, wood, and steel
- liquid, like water and oil
- gas, such as air, methane, and helium

These are all **states of matter**.

Energy causes change. Heat is a type of energy. When you heat a solid object, it **expands**, or gets bigger. When a solid object cools it gets smaller, or it **contracts**.

Liquids and gases expand in the same way when they are heated.

On warm days metal bridges expand. They are built with a gap at each end. This stops the bridge bending and cracking in hot weather.

water vapour water in the form of a gas

Changing state

Enough energy can change matter from one state to another.

If you heat ice, it becomes water. The heat changes a solid into a liquid. If you heat the water, it becomes **water vapour**. This is a gas, so heat changes a liquid into a gas.

Water vapour can be changed back to a liquid by cooling it.

There she blows
This is the Strokkur **geyser** in Iceland. Hot water and water vapour shoot 30 metres (100 feet) into the air.

geyser   opening where water and water vapour shoot out of the ground

Solids

Fossils

This fish died millions of years ago. Its body was buried at the bottom of a lake. The solid parts, like the bones, kept their shape and **volume**. Over thousands of years they turned into rock.

What is a solid?

A solid keeps its shape. It does not need a container to hold it in. A solid takes up the same amount of space wherever it is. Wood, stone, and plastic are all solid materials.

A solid is made up of **particles**. In a solid they are tightly packed together. You cannot easily push particles of a solid aside. That is why you cannot walk through a brick wall.

Some artists make ice sculptures from large blocks of ice. They have to chip off or saw away the ice.

conduction movement of heat or electricity from one particle to another in a solid

Conducting heat

Conduction is how heat moves through solids.
Heat **energy** passes from particle to particle.
Copper is a good **conductor** of heat and electricity.
It is used for home wiring and to make pans.
Plastics are poor conductors of heat. They are used
to **insulate** wires and they make good pan handles.

Did you know?

Diamonds and graphite are both forms of carbon. Diamonds are very hard. Graphite is used in pencils. It is soft and slippery.

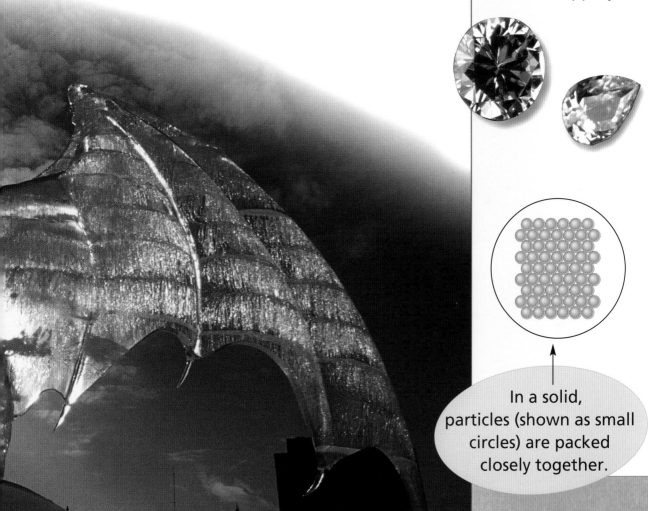

In a solid, particles (shown as small circles) are packed closely together.

Solids with crystals

The **particles** in **crystals** are laid out in a regular pattern. Crystals have straight edges and smooth sides. When you break a crystal, a flat surface is left. Salt, snowflakes, and diamonds are made up of crystals.

Most crystals form when a liquid cools. The size of the crystals depends on how quickly the liquid cools. Crystals will be larger if the liquid cools slowly.

Diamonds

Diamond crystals have smooth, straight surfaces. Diamonds break neatly along these surfaces. This makes it easier for diamond cutters to 'cut' diamonds for jewellery.

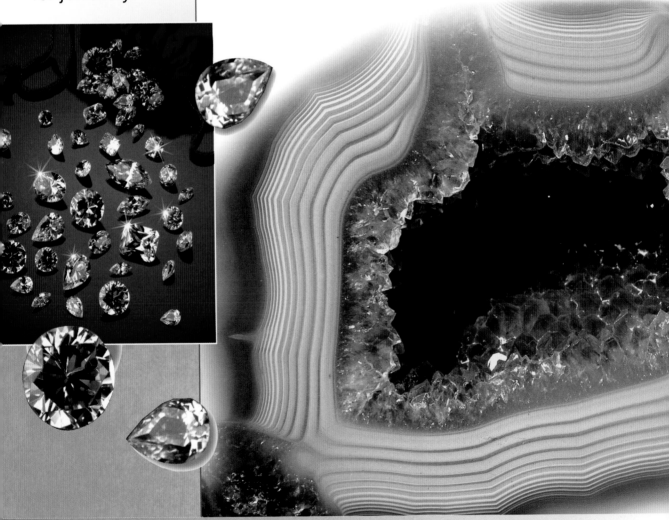

crystal solid with particles laid out in a regular pattern

Solids without shape

The particles in some solids are not laid out in a regular pattern. They are not made up of crystals. Chocolate, butter, candle wax, and glass are like this.

Solids that are made up of crystals **melt** all at once at a certain temperature. Solids that are not made up of crystals melt little by little. Chocolate gets softer and softer as it melts.

Obsidian
When **lava** from a volcano cools very quickly, obsidian is made. When obsidian breaks, the broken surface is curved and is very sharp.

Quartz crystals all have the same shape. But they can be colourless, pink, purple, yellow, or brown.

lava molten rock that has risen to the Earth's surface

Solids around us

Solids are everywhere. **Steel** is an important solid. Steel is used to make many things. Steel is iron with small amounts of other materials added to it.

There are many types of steel. High-carbon steel is very strong. It is used in railway tracks.

Stainless steel does not rust. It is used to make kitchen and hospital equipment.

Steel frames
This building has a steel frame rather than a wooden frame. They are safer in fires and winds.

The Red Fort in Delhi, India was built from a rock called sandstone.

steel iron with small amounts of other substances added to it

Rocks

Rocks are solids. Granite and limestone are hard rocks. They are good for building houses and walls. Slate can be used for roofs and floors.

If you heat clay with crushed limestone, it makes cement. Cement is used as the 'glue' to lay bricks when building walls. It is also used for making **concrete**.

Lighter cars

The body panels of these cars are made from plastic and glass fibres. The cars are strong and light. So they need less fuel to move them along.

concrete mixture of cement with sand and crushed stones

Liquids

Liquids do not have a shape of their own. They take the shape of the container they are in. Liquids do have a definite **volume**. A litre of milk takes up a litre of space — whether it is in a glass or if it is spilled on the floor. It is very difficult to squeeze liquids into a smaller volume. They will not stretch out to fill a large space either.

Particles in a liquid

The **particles** in a liquid are not as close together as they are in a solid. They move around each other easily. This is why a liquid can flow.

Drops of metal

Mercury is a metal. Unusually for a metal it is a liquid at **room temperature**. When it is spilled, mercury forms droplets, like those below.

Here, water takes the shape of the stream. When it flows into the lake it takes the shape of the lake.

room temperature about 20 °C (68 °F)

Heat in liquids

Heat **energy** spreads quickly through liquids. It does this by a process called **convection**. When a pan of water is heated on a stove, the water at the bottom of the pan becomes warm. The warm water rises. The cold water sinks and takes its place. This movement spreads the heat through the water.

Pouring liquids

Some liquids flow or pour more easily than others do. Water is very easy to pour. Honey pours slowly. Tar is almost impossible to pour!

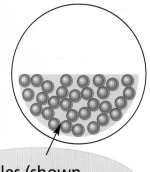

Particles (shown as small circles) can move around each other easily in a liquid.

convection spread of heat through a liquid or gas

Slippery oil

Lubricating oil comes from crude oil. It helps the moving parts of machines to slide past each other easily. Motor oil is very important for car engines to run properly.

Tractors, trucks, and some cars run on diesel fuel.

Liquids around us

Water is the most important liquid around us. We would die without it. Other liquids are important too. Oil is an important liquid. It is used to make electricity and to heat our homes.

Crude oil

When oil is found deep underground, it is a dark, thick liquid. It is called crude oil. Petrol, diesel fuel, and **lubricating** oils all come from crude oil.

lubricating making slippery. This helps to reduce wear and tear.

Other important liquids

You will find many liquids around the home. These might be paints, **detergents**, or medicines. Many foods, like milk, fruit juice, and honey are liquids.

Acids are important liquids too. Vinegar is a weak acid. Lemons and apples contain weak acids. Some acids are strong. Hydrochloric acid is a strong acid. It is in our stomachs. It helps us to **digest** our food.

Thermometers

Thermometers are used to measure temperature. They are narrow tubes that are filled with liquid. When the temperature goes up, the liquid rises up the tube. The level falls as the liquid gets colder.

Most thermometers contain alcohol. Colour is added to the alcohol, so we can see it.

Gases

Gases have no shape of their own. They take the shape of the container they are put into. Because of this, air has a different shape in a ball and in a tyre. But the **volume** of a gas changes too. Gas **particles** spread out to fill all the space there is.

Gas particles

Gas particles are much further apart than particles in a liquid. Gas particles move all the time. They bounce off each other and the walls of their container.

Carrying air

Firefighters carry tanks that have had air squeezed into them. The firefighters breathe this air instead of the thick, **toxic** smoke that is in burning buildings.

When a car crashes, gas is released into the air bags. It quickly fills the air bags and takes their shape.

Word bank   toxic can harm or kill you, like a poison

Gases and heat

Heat travels through gases like it travels through liquids, by **convection**. Hot air rises. Cold air flows in to take its place. The cold air heats up too and also rises. In this way a circular **current** of air is formed. It carries heat around the room.

A spray can, like this, spreads sweet-smelling gases across a room in just a few minutes. This is because gas particles move about so much.

Gases under pressure

If you squeeze a balloon filled with gas, the gas inside pushes back. It produces a **force**. This happens because the gas **particles** bump into each other or the walls of their container. **Pressure** is the force of the gas particles on a certain **area** of a surface.

Barometers

A barometer measures the pressure of the air around us. This tells us what the weather will be like.

The arrow on this barometer has moved all the way to 'very dry'. This means the air pressure is high.

pressure force put on a certain area of surface

Volume and pressure

When gas particles are far apart, few of them hit the walls of their container. The pressure they produce is small. When gas is in a small space, the particles are pushed closer together. Then they hit the container walls more often. They exert a greater pressure.

Pump the same amount of air into a large tyre as into a small tyre. The pressure of the large tyre will be lower than the pressure of the small tyre.

Putting out fires

Gases can turn into liquids if they are put under very high pressure. Inside this fire extinguisher is liquid carbon dioxide. It is under very high pressure. When the liquid is let out, the carbon dioxide returns to normal pressure. It turns back into a gas.

This firefighter is using a carbon dioxide gas extinguisher to put out a fire.

area amount of surface

Volume and temperature

Blow up a balloon and tie it closed. Then run cold water over it. What happens? It gets smaller, or **contracts**. If you place it under warm water, the balloon will **expand** or get bigger.

Balloons have stretchy walls. The walls of the balloon can move outwards. This happens when the **volume** of the gas inside gets bigger. The walls move inwards when the volume of the gas inside gets smaller.

Check the tyre pressure!

Tyres have stretchy walls, like balloons. When the air temperature is cold the volume of the air inside the tyre gets smaller. The tyre goes down slightly.

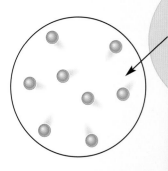

Particles (shown as small circles) in a gas move around freely. They take up all the space there is.

Word bank   volume amount of space something takes up

Temperature and pressure

Plastic tanks may contain a gas, like air. The walls of a plastic tank will not stretch. They are **rigid**. So what happens when the gas gets warmer? The volume of the gas cannot change. The gas particles hit the tank's walls more often and with more **force**. The **pressure** of the gas gets higher.

If the gas is cooled, the gas particles move slowly again. The pressure drops.

The pressure of a gas in a rigid container depends on its temperature.

Scuba tanks

The air in scuba tanks is under very high pressure. Scuba tanks must not be left in cars on a hot day. The air pressure in the tank would rise even higher. The tank might explode.

The burner flame is heating the air in this hot air balloon. The air expands and its volume increases. The balloon **inflates**.

rigid stiff, not able to stretch or bend

The Earth's atmosphere

There is a layer of gases around the Earth. This is called the **atmosphere**. Near the Earth, it is often called air. We only notice air when it is windy. But life would be impossible without air.

Air contains many gases. But two of them make up most of the air. Nitrogen makes up 78 per cent of air. Oxygen makes up 21 per cent. Other gases make up 1 per cent of air.

Water vapour in the air

In a tropical rainforest the air feels hot and damp. Rainforest air looks misty. This is because it contains so much **water vapour**.

Oxygen 21% — Other gases 1%

Nitrogen 78%

atmosphere layer of gases around a planet like Earth

Air pressure

The gases in the air push down on the Earth. Air **pressure** is the **force** of the air on the Earth's surface.

The force of the air pushing down on us does not crush our bodies. The gases and liquids in our bodies push back with the same pressure as the air pressure outside.

Climbing high!

High up in the mountains there is less air above us to push down. The air pressure is lower. The air contains less oxygen. Most mountain climbers breathe from a tank with oxygen in it.

The atmosphere protects living things from the Sun's harmful rays.

force push or pull

The atmosphere close to Earth

The **atmosphere** is divided into layers. The troposhere is closest to the Earth. Most of the Earth's weather happens in this layer.

The next layer up is the stratosphere. Jet planes often fly in this layer. The stratosphere contains **ozone**. Ozone protects living things from the Sun's harmful rays. Without ozone the Sun's rays would kill most living things on the Earth.

Giant balloons

Scientists send giant balloons into the stratosphere to learn more about this layer. As the balloon gets further from Earth the air **pressure** gets less so the balloon expands.

The **volume** of weather balloons can increase more than 250 times in the stratosphere.

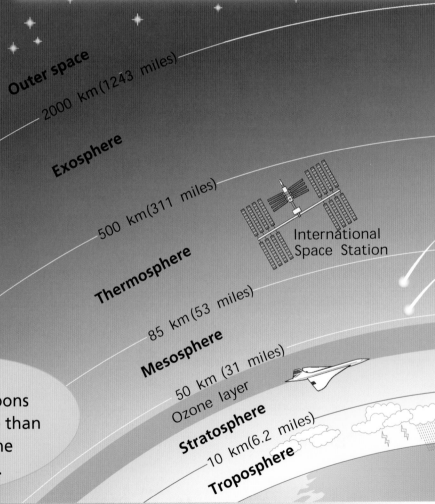

Outer space

2000 km (1243 miles)

Exosphere

500 km (311 miles)

Thermosphere

International Space Station

85 km (53 miles)

Mesosphere

50 km (31 miles)

Ozone layer

Stratosphere

10 km (6.2 miles)

Troposhere

ozone form of oxygen that absorbs the Sun's harmful rays

Further from the Earth

The mesosphere is the middle layer. **Meteorites** from other planets burn up in this layer. A shooting star is a meteorite burning up in the mesosphere.

The thermosphere is near the outside of the atmosphere. The International Space Station moves around the Earth in the thermosphere.

The outer layer of the atmosphere is the exosphere. The exosphere goes on to where outer space begins.

The Space Shuttle travelled around the Earth in the thermosphere and the exosphere. The Space Shuttle used small bursts of gas from rockets to move around.

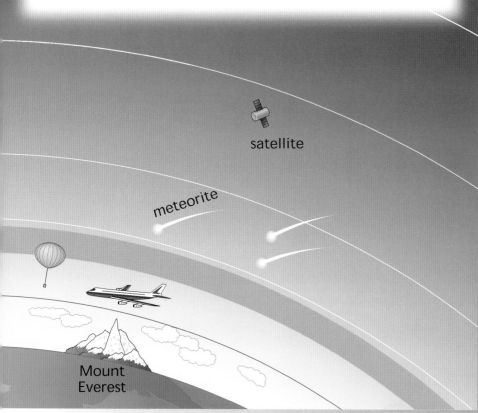

satellite

meteorite

Mount Everest

meteorite solid object that enters the Earth's atmosphere from outer space

Plasmas

Giant spark of electricity

Lightning travels through the air and heats up the gases. The air can become hotter than 27,000°C (49,000°F). Its gases turn into plasma.

Did you know there is a fourth **state of matter**? It is called **plasma**. If gases are heated enough they can become plasmas.

Gas **particles** move faster when they are heated. When they become very hot, they bump into each other with a huge **force**. Then the gas particles break up into tinier particles. These tiny particles make up plasma.

This is the Cat's Eye Nebula. The small dark spots are clumps of dust and gas.

plasma mixture of tiny particles at a high temperature that carry electricity

Where plasmas are found

Plasmas are not common on Earth. But there are plenty in the **universe**. Space contains a lot of gas and dust. The gas and dust clumps together. A huge cloud of gas and dust is called a **nebula**. Inside a nebula it gets very hot. The gases turn into plasma. Stars form from the plasma in nebulas. All stars, including our Sun, are made up of plasma.

Plasma lights
This is a neon light. It is a gas tube filled with neon gas. Electricity passes through the gas. The gas changes into glowing plasma.

Changes in state

The state of a substance depends on its temperature. If you cool a liquid enough it will change to a solid state. This is called **freezing**. When you fill an ice-cube tray with water and place it in a freezer, it turns to a solid.

As a liquid cools, its **particles** move closer together. When they get very close together they form a solid. The liquid freezes. Water freezes at 0 °C (32 °F) — this is its **freezing point**.

Molten mountain

This is a volcano erupting in Hawaii. Liquid rock or **lava** bursts out from deep inside the Earth. When the lava cools, it changes state and becomes solid.

freeze change from a liquid to a solid

Melting

The particles of a solid move faster when a solid is heated. When the particles can move around each other, the solid changes to a liquid. This is called **melting**. Ice melts at 0° C (32° F).

Notice that water melts and freezes at the same temperature. This is true for all substances.

Playing on ice
Ice hockey is one of several popular sports played upon frozen water.

This iron melted at 1535° C (2795° F). It will freeze when it cools to the same temperature.

melt change from a solid to a liquid

Frost

In very cold air water vapour can change straight into ice **crystals**. This is frost.

Evaporation

Why does the water in puddles slowly disappear? The water at the surface of the puddle changes into **water vapour**. It slowly escapes from the liquid into the air. This is called **evaporation**.

Boiling

If a liquid is heated enough, it changes to a gas quickly. Bubbles of gas keep forming under the liquid's surface. The bubbles rise to the surface and escape. The liquid is **boiling**. Water boils at 100° C (212° F).

evaporation process when a liquid changes to a gas

Condensation

After a hot bath you may see mist on the bathroom mirror. This happens because the warm water **particles** (water vapour) in the air hit the cold mirror. The cold mirror cools the water vapour. It changes into mist. Mist is a liquid. The water vapour has **condensed**.

Water evaporates from this hot spring. But in the cold air the water vapour condenses into tiny droplets and forms mist.

Engine vapour lock

In hot weather petrol **evaporates**. Petrol gas or vapour partly fills a car's fuel tank. A car's fuel pump cannot pump gas. So petrol does not reach the engine. This means the car will not start.

condense change from a gas to a liquid

Fluids in action

Objects seem to weigh less when they are in water. This is because the water pushes up on the object. It applies a **force**.

Water is a **fluid**. All liquids and gases are fluids. When fluids touch a surface, they apply a force.

Floating and sinking

A ship floats. The force of the water pushing up is more than the force of the ship pushing down.

Fish

Fish need to control how much they float. Fish have swim bladders. A swim bladder is a sac filled with air. The fish put more air into the swim bladder to rise and let air out to sink.

Word bank   fluid any matter that flows. Liquids and gases are fluids.

Pumping fluids

A plastic bottle is full of water with its lid on. It is a closed container. The water has nowhere to go.

Now take the cap off the top of the bottle and squeeze. The water will shoot out of the top.

When you squeezed the bottle, you applied a force. This is called a force pump.

A ship floats because it is hollow. It is mostly air!

Pumping blood

The human heart has two force pumps. One pump pushes blood from the heart to the lungs. There the blood picks up oxygen. The other pump pushes the oxygen-filled blood to the rest of the body.

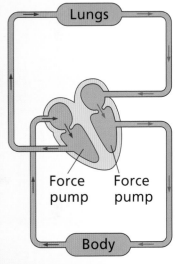

Lungs

Force pump

Force pump

Body

Pneumatic drills,
like this, are used
to break up
concrete. They are
powered by air
under pressure.

Fluids contained

Liquids will not squeeze into a smaller space.
So, what happens when you squeeze a full bottle
of water with the cap still on? The water pushes
back with the same **pressure**. But it pushes back
over the whole surface of the plastic bottle; not
just the small part you squeezed. This means
that fluids, like water, pass on force to all parts
of the fluid.

A person can lift a
car with the help of
a hydraulic jack.

hydraulic system that works by passing pressure through
a fluid

Hydraulics

A fluid in a closed container can make a small force larger. **Hydraulic** systems make use of this **property**.

Mechanics use a machine called a hydraulic jack. A person pumps a handle. This puts a small force on a small **piston**. This force passes through a fluid and on to a bigger piston with a large **area**. The fluid pushes on the large area. It makes a big force. This is how a small force can lift a heavy car.

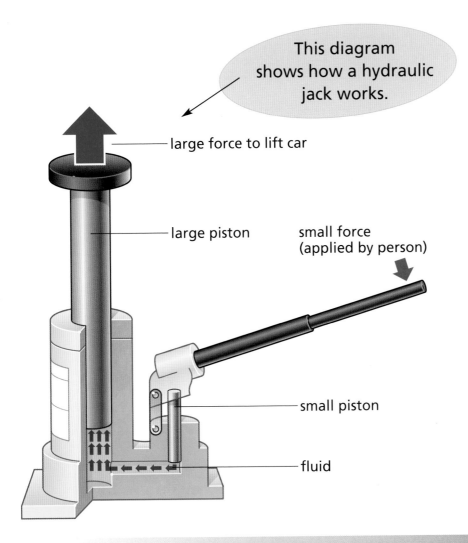

This diagram shows how a hydraulic jack works.

large force to lift car

large piston

small force (applied by person)

small piston

fluid

piston metal cylinder that fits closely inside a tube. Pistons are important parts of car engines and other machines.

Weird water

Water heats and cools slowly

Places near the sea are not as hot as places further **inland**. They are also not as cold in the winter as places further inland.

On Earth, you can find water as ice, liquid water, and **water vapour**. We find water in all three **states of matter**. In nature there is no other substance like this.

You can find water in its solid state as:
• snow, **sleet**, and **hail**
• ice on lakes, ponds, rivers, and streams
• ice caps and **glaciers**.

You can find water in its liquid state in:
• oceans, rivers, and lakes
• wetlands, like marshes and swamps
• living things.

You can find water in its gas state as:
• water vapour in the **atmosphere**.

sleet pellets of ice

Ice floats!

Usually a substance in its solid form is heavier than its liquid form. For example, solid iron would sink in liquid iron. But water is not like other substances. Ice floats in water.

As water cools its **particles** get closer together. But when water cools below 4° C (39° F) the particles move apart again. Empty spaces form between the particles. At 0° C (32° F) the **expanded** liquid **freezes** and becomes ice.

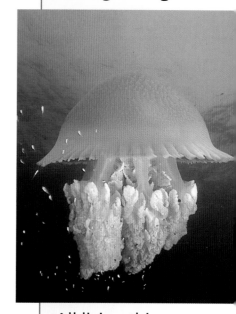

All living things contain water. This is the largest jellyfish. It is called the Lion's Mane and it is about 2.5 metres (8 feet) across. Jellyfish are over 90 per cent water.

Icebergs float in the ocean. But only one tenth of the iceberg is above water.

glacier large mass of snow and ice that moves slowly

The Earth's water

Water covers about three-quarters of the Earth's surface. Only 3 per cent of this water is fresh. Some of the things we need fresh water for are drinking, washing, growing crops, and power stations. But two thirds of the fresh water on Earth is frozen as ice. It cannot be used. This means we can only use 1 per cent of the Earth's water supply.

Groundwater

There is far more fresh water under the ground than in lakes and rivers. To get at **groundwater** people have to drill wells. The water is pumped to the surface.

This drilling rig can drill through solid rock to get water.

The oceans contain 97 per cent of the Earth's water. This water is too salty for us to use.

Word bank   groundwater water that has collected underground

The water cycle

The Earth's water changes and moves all the time. This is called the **water cycle**. Heat from the Sun **evaporates** water from oceans, rivers, and lakes. **Water vapour** rises into the air. It cools and turns back into liquid water, making clouds. Water then falls as rain, **hail**, or snow. Water runs off the land into streams and rivers. It flows back into lakes and oceans.

condensation

rain, snow, or hail

evaporation

heated by the Sun

water runs off land into oceans

Plants and the water cycle

Plants need water to grow. Their roots take up water from the ground. Plants lose water through their leaves as water vapour. This goes back into the air.

Find out more

Websites
BBC Science
News, features, and activities on science.
www.bbc.co.uk

Creative Chemistry
Fun, practical activities, quizzes, puzzles, and more.
www.creative-chemistry.org.uk

skoool.co.uk
Help for science projects and homework.
http://kent.skoool.co.uk/

Books

Discovering Science: Matter, Rebecca Hunter (Raintree, 2003)
Solids, Liquids, Gases, Charnon Simon (Compass Point Books, 2000)
The Water Cycle, Theresa Greenaway (Raintree, 2001)

World Wide Web

To find out more about states of matter you can search the Internet. Use keywords like these:

- "states of matter"
- solids +liquids +gases
- water +evaporation +condensation

You can find your own keywords by using words from this book. The search tips below will help you find useful websites.

Search tips

There are billions of pages on the Internet. It can be difficult to find exactly what you are looking for. These tips will help you find useful websites more quickly:

- know what you want to find out about
- use simple keywords
- use two to six keywords in a search
- only use names of people, places or things
- put double quote marks around words that go together, for example "states of matter"

Where to search
Search engine
A search engine looks through through millions of website pages. It lists all the sites that match the words in the search box. You will find the best matches are at the top of the list, on the first page.

Search directory
A person instead of a computer has sorted a search directory. You can search by keyword or subject and browse through the different sites. It is like looking through books on a library shelf.

Glossary

acid chemical that contains hydrogen. Acids have a sour taste and can burn you.

area amount of surface

atmosphere layer of gases around a planet like Earth

atom tiny particle that makes up all matter

boil rapid change of state from a liquid to a gas that takes place within the liquid as well as at its surface

concrete mixture of cement with sand and crushed stones

condensation when a gas turns into a liquid

condense change from a gas to a liquid

conduction movement of heat or electricity from one particle to another in a solid

conductor material through which heat or electricity passes easily

contract become smaller in size; take up less space

convection spread of heat through a liquid or gas

crystal solid with particles laid out in a regular pattern

current flow of gas or liquid

deflate let air or gas out of an object

detergent liquid used with water to remove dirt

digest break down food so it can be used by the body

energy ability to cause change

evaporate change from a liquid to a gas

evaporation process when a liquid changes to a gas

expand become larger in size; take up more space

fluid any matter that flows. Liquids and gases are fluids.

force push or pull

freeze change from a liquid to a solid

freezing point temperature at which a substance changes from a liquid to a solid

geyser opening where water and water vapour shoot out of the ground

glacier large mass of snow and ice that moves slowly

groundwater water that has collected underground

hail water falling from clouds as small pieces of ice

hydraulic system that works by passing pressure through a fluid

inflate fill an object with gas

inland land that is far from the sea

insulate stop heat and electricity moving through a material

lava molten rock that has risen to the Earth's surface

lubricating making slippery. This helps to reduce wear and tear.

mass amount of matter in an object

matter anything that takes up space and has mass

melt change from a solid to a liquid

meteorite solid object that enters the Earth's atmosphere from outer space

nebula cloud of dust and gas in outer space

ozone form of oxygen that absorbs the Sun's harmful rays

particle small part of something

piston metal cylinder that fits closely inside a tube. Pistons are important parts of car engines and other machines.

plasma mixture of tiny particles at a high temperature that carry electricity

pneumatic powered by high-pressure air

pressure force put on a certain area of surface

property feature of something

reaction chemical change that produces new substances

rigid stiff, not able to stretch or bend

room temperature about 20 °C (68 °F)

sleet pellets of ice

state of matter whether something is solid, liquid, gas, or plasma

steel iron with small amounts of other substances added to it

thermostat instrument used to control temperature

toxic can harm or kill you, like a poison

universe everything that exists

volume amount of space that something takes up

water cycle movement of water between the air, land, and sea

water vapour water in the form of a gas

Index

Titles in the Freestyle Express: Material Matters series include:

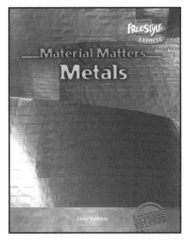

Hardback   1 844 43356 0

Hardback   1 844 43357 9

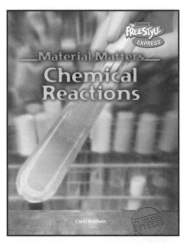

Hardback   1 844 43358 7

Hardback   1 844 43381 1

Hardback   1 844 43382 X

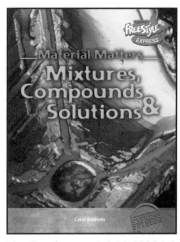

Hardback   1 844 43601 2

Find out about other Freestyle Express titles on our website www.raintreepublishers.co.uk